SCIENTIFIC AMERICAN EDUCATIONAL PUBLISHING

DESIGN & BUILD IT

10 FUN ENGINEERING PROJECTS

BRING SCIENCE HOME

Published in 2023 by Scientific American Educational Publishing in association with The Rosen Publishing Group
29 East 21st Street, New York, NY 10010

Contains material from Scientific American , a division of Springer Nature America, Inc., reprinted by permission as well as original material from The Rosen Publishing Group .

First Edition

Designer: Rachel Rising

Activity on page 9 by Science Buddies/Ben Finio; page 13 Science Buddies/Sabine De Brabandere; page 17 by Science Buddies/Ben Finio; page 23 by Science Buddies/Ben Finio; page 27 Science Buddies/Ben Finio; page 33 Science Buddies/Ben Finio; page 43 Science Buddies/Ben Finio; page 49 Science Buddies/Ben Finio; page 55 Science Buddies.

Illustrations by Continuum Content Solutions

Photo Credits: pp. 5, 7, 9, 12, 17, 23, 27, 33, 37, 43, 49, 55 Anna Frajtova/Shutterstock.com; pp. 5, 7, 9, 12, 17, 23, 27, 33, 37, 43, 49, 55 cve iv/Shutterstock.com.

Cataloging-in-Publication Data
Names: Scientific American, inc.
Title: Design & build it : 10 fun engineering projects / edited by the Editors of Scientific American.
Description: New York : Scientific American Educational Publishing, 2023. | Series: Bring science home | Includes glossary and index.
Identifiers: ISBN 9781684169573 (pbk.) | ISBN 9781684169580 (library bound) | ISBN 9781684169597 (ebook)
Subjects: LCSH: Engineering--Experiments--Juvenile literature. | Science projects--Juvenile literature.
Classification: LCC TA149.D475 2023 | DDC 620.0078--dc23

Manufactured in the United States of America

CPSIA Compliance Information: Batch #SACS23. For further information contact Rosen Publishing, New York, New York at 1-800-237-9932.

SCIENTIFIC AMERICAN. EDUCATIONAL PUBLISHING

DESIGN & BUILD IT

10 FUN ENGINEERING PROJECTS

BRING SCIENCE HOME

CONTENTS

THESE ACTIVITIES INCLUDE SCIENCE FAIR PROJECT IDEAS.

INTRODUCTION

You might be surprised by how many of the things we use every day rely on engineering! Just about anything people build is first designed by engineers. Using basic craft materials, you can try your hand at engineering too. Build a catapult, a bridge, an artificial hand that can pick up objects, and much more!

Projects marked with include a section called Science Fair Project ideas. These ideas can help you develop your own original science fair project. Science fair judges tend to reward creative thought and imagination, and it helps if you are really interested in your project. You will also need to follow the scientific method. See page 61 for more information about that.

Build a Recycling-Sorting Machine

USE SIMPLE SCIENCE TO TEST HOW RECYCLING CENTERS MIGHT SORT OUR CAST-OFF MATERIALS—AND BUILD YOUR OWN SORTING MACHINE!

Does your community have single-stream recycling, which allows you to mix materials into one recycling container? Have you ever wondered how those materials all get separated so they can be recycled into new things? Try this activity to find out as you build your own recycling-sorting machine!

PROJECT TIME

60 to 90 minutes

KEY CONCEPTS

Material properties
Forces
Weight
Magnetism
Recycling
Engineering

BACKGROUND

Recycling allows our old plastics, glass, aluminum, and papers to be broken down and turned into new things. For example, plastic bottles might be melted down and turned into park benches or playground equipment, and old paper can be turned into new paper towels or napkins. Many communities in the U.S. now offer single-stream recycling. This allows you to mix your different types of recyclables into a single container for collection.

That process presents a challenge, however. Before the materials can actually be recycled, they need to be separated and sorted. You don't want bits of plastic or metal in your recycled paper towels! After recyclables are collected, they get transported by trucks to recycling plants called materials recovery facilities (MRFs). In MRFs, giant piles of mixed materials are fed through machines that separate them out into different categories and bundle them to be shipped off to processing plants. Much of the sorting is done automatically by machines that make clever use of different properties of the materials. Magnets, for example, can attract metal objects, and blowing air can separate lighter paper and cardboard from heavier objects such as glass bottles and metal cans.

This process is not without its downsides. Plastic bags can clog sorting machines, which is why they typically cannot be included in single-stream recycling. Many communities only accept certain types of plastic, and they require that food containers be rinsed thoroughly before being placed in the recycling. Ignoring these guidelines can result in contamination of the recycled materials, making them unusable—so they will still wind up in the trash! This is why it's very important to make sure you follow your community's recycling guidelines.

In this project you will focus on separating two materials: shreds of paper and paper clips. Can you build a machine to separate them efficiently? Try it and find out!

MATERIALS

- At least two dozen paper clips
- Paper
- Scissors
- Magnets
- Flat workspace, such as a tabletop
- Cups or other small containers
- Construction materials such as cardboard, plastic bottles, tape and/or other craft supplies that you can use to build a recycling-sorting machine
- Additional items to sort, such as glass and plastic marbles or large and small plastic beads

PREPARATION

- Carefully cut a few dozen pieces of paper into roughly 1-inch by 1-inch (2.5 cm by 2.5 cm) pieces (they can be irregular shapes of this size). This will be quicker if you fold the paper first so you can cut multiple pieces at once.

- Put the paper pieces in a cup with the paper clips. Cover the top of the cup with your hand so nothing falls out, and shake the cup to mix them.

PROCEDURE

- Dump the mixed paper clips and paper pieces into a pile onto your work surface. Try separating them manually. *How long does it take you to pick them apart by hand?*

- Remix the paper clips and paper pieces, then dump them back on the table. Try using air to separate them by blowing on them. *Is this method easier or harder than sorting by hand?*

- Remix and dump the materials again. This time try separating them using a magnet. *Can you completely separate them all using just a magnet?*

- Real recycling plants use a combination of different methods to separate materials. Using what you've learned from your tests, can you build a machine that will separate a mixed cup of paper clips and paper pieces into two different piles or cups? One method (but certainly not the only way) is to build a ramp and/or a funnel that is lined with magnets on the outside. When you pour the mixed cup of paper clips and paper pieces into the machine, they all slide down. The paper clips should get stuck to the magnets in the walls, and the paper continues to fall. Try building this machine out of your construction materials. *How effective do you think it will be?*

- Test out your machine. *How effective was it? Do any paper clips fall through to the bottom, or do any shreds of paper get stuck by the magnets? How could you improve your machine?*
- Try making any changes to your machine that might help it be more effective, then redo the sorting test.

SCIENCE FAIR IDEA

Try this project with different materials. *Can you sort objects by weight or by size? For example, what about glass marbles and plastic marbles or large and small plastic beads?*

OBSERVATIONS AND RESULTS

You probably found moderate success if you built a ramp-and-funnel-style device with magnets to separate the paper clips and paper shreds. It might be difficult to build a device that can completely separate the materials without some manual sorting. Some paper clips may whiz by the magnets without getting stuck. As more paper clips start sticking to the magnets, they can create clogs where shreds of paper get trapped. This results in two sets of materials that are better than what you started with, but still not completely separated—it probably required some manual sorting to finish the job.

Real recycling plants have moving conveyor belts and powerful electromagnets that can be turned on and off. This lets them pull magnetic materials up off the conveyor belt and move them away, separating them from nonmagnetic materials such as plastic, glass and paper, and reducing their chances of getting stuck together.

CLEANUP

You can recycle your paper pieces, but note that paper clips generally cannot be recycled in normal curbside collection recycling—you can reuse them at home instead.

Gravity-Powered Sorting Machine

WANT TO SORT THROUGH OBJECTS OF DIFFERENT SIZES QUICKLY? ENGINEER A SIMPLE MACHINE TO DO IT FOR YOU!

Have you ever used a coin-sorting machine to separate pennies, nickels, dimes, and quarters? When you need to separate things that are all mixed together, using a machine can be much faster than picking them apart by hand. In this project, you will build a machine that can automatically separate two different size marbles—powered by nothing but gravity!

PROJECT TIME

45 to 50 minutes

KEY CONCEPTS

Physics
Engineering
Gravity
Mechanical design

BACKGROUND

Sorting machines are used in many different applications, but they all have something in common. They automate a task that would be time-consuming or even impossible to do by hand. It might not be that difficult to sort a pocketful of coins manually, but what if you worked at a bank and had to sort thousands of coins? It would be nice to have a machine to do it! Mining is another example. Early miners would use a manual process called panning to separate gold nuggets from dirt and sand in a pan. Today, huge industrial machines are used to separate valuable gems and minerals from other rocks and dirt. Many recycling facilities have machines that can automatically separate paper, plastic, and metal objects—meaning that if your town has single-stream recycling, you can just dump all your recyclables into one bin at home, without sorting them yourself!

How exactly do machines separate all these different materials? They make use of the fact that different objects and materials have different properties. For example, some materials are magnetic and some are not, so you can use magnets to separate magnetic and nonmagnetic materials. Materials have different densities—meaning some will float in water and some will sink. Some will be easily blown away by a strong puff of air, while others are heavy enough to stay put. Objects have many different sizes and shapes. Some might have smooth, round shapes that let them roll easily (such as a ball), and others might have irregular or flat shapes that make them get stuck easily (such as a flat piece of cardboard). Smaller objects can fall through holes in a grate, while larger objects get stuck on top of it. In this project, you will make use of that last feature to separate marbles with two different diameters.

MATERIALS

- Plastic cups
- Craft sticks
- Paper
- Tape
- Glue
- Scissors
- A few dozen small marbles or plastic or wooden beads from a craft store. A diameter of roughly 0.25 inch (6 mm) works well.
- A few dozen large marbles, or plastic or wooden beads from a craft store. A diameter of roughly 0.5 inch (12 mm) works well.

PREPARATION

- Pour a mixture of both large and small marbles into a single plastic cup. Shake or stir the cup to make sure the marbles are well mixed.

- The goal of this project is to build a machine where you can pour a mixed cup of large and small marbles into one end and have the machine automatically sort them into two different cups by size. This is an engineering design project, meaning there is no single "right" way to do this. The procedure will describe one possible approach, but don't be afraid to modify it or try your own idea!

PROCEDURE

- Glue several craft sticks together to form a grate, as shown in the illustration on page 13. The gaps between the sticks should be large enough that the small marbles can fit through them, but small enough that the large marbles cannot.

- Use plastic cups, other craft sticks, paper, glue, and tape to build a support structure for your grate to hold it at an angle above two plastic cups. (If you use tape, you might be able to easily take apart your machine if you decide you want to modify it later. Using glue might make this trickier—but you can build additional machines if necessary.) One cup should be directly below the grate to collect the smaller marbles as they fall through; the other cup should be at the lower end of the grate to collect the larger marbles. Make sure the collection cups are not permanently attached to the rest of the machine—you need to be able to remove them easily.

- Roll up a piece of paper or carefully cut up a plastic cup, and use it to make a funnel at the top end of your grate so you have a place to pour the marbles into your machine.

- Pour your cup of mixed marbles into the funnel and watch what happens. *How do the marbles flow through your machine? Do the smaller marbles fall through the grate?*

- Now, remove the two collection cups and look at their contents. *Are the cups perfectly sorted (all large marbles in one, all small marbles in the other) or are they "contaminated" with some marbles in the wrong cups?*
- Pour all the marbles back into a single cup and mix them again.
- Engineers rarely get things perfect on the first try. "Iteration" is an important part of the engineering design process—meaning you design something, build it, test it, then go back and repeat the process to improve the design. *If your collection cups were contaminated with the wrong marbles, how can you improve your design so it works better?*
- Try improving or changing your design so you can sort all the marbles into the correct cups. *Can you get to the point where your samples are perfectly sorted, with all the marbles in the right cups?*

OBSERVATIONS AND RESULTS

It is unlikely that you will build a machine that works perfectly on the first try. In particular, some of the smaller marbles might roll too quickly across the grate while staying on the flat side of a craft stick, never falling through one of the holes, so they wind up in the wrong cup. There are multiple ways you could fix this. You can make the grate longer to increase the odds that the small marbles will fall through a hole. You can tilt the craft sticks or put them on edge so the flat sides are not sitting horizontally, so the smaller marbles will always roll down toward the holes. You can put other craft stick pieces perpendicular to the rest of the grate to serve as obstacles, causing the marbles to bounce around as they roll down—again, increasing the odds that the small ones will fall through the holes. Once you improve your grate, you should be able to build a machine that can perfectly sort the large and small marbles. It can also help if you pour the marbles into the machine slowly instead of dumping them in all at once.

CLEANUP

Check the floor to make sure you did not drop any marbles (they can be a choking or trip hazard).

Gear Up Your Candy

GEARS GO 'ROUND: PUT YOUR EXTRA CANDY TO USE CREATING GEARS THAT SPIN—SOMETIMES IN SURPRISING WAYS!

Did you know that gears are all around you? You can find them in wind-up toys, bicycles, carousels, cars and trucks, cranes, drills, wind turbines, analog watches, and so forth! If you've looked closely at a moving bicycle, you have seen gears at work. Are you curious about their purpose? In this activity, you will use candy to make gears and explore why they are so versatile.

PROJECT TIME

30 to 40 minutes

KEY CONCEPTS

Physics
Engineering
Gears
Mechanics

BACKGROUND

A gear is a special type of wheel. It is a disk that has teeth called cogs around its edge. Most of the time the teeth of two gears interlock, making the two wheels turn together. Sometimes the teeth mesh with a chain that connects the gears. You have probably seen this setup in bicycles.

Gears make tasks easier for humans and for motors. In many machines, humans or motors make an axle (a rod that runs through a wheel or gear) turn, and the right gears can make the turning more efficient.

Choosing the right combination of gears is the key to efficient work. Some bikes allow you to choose gears. Depending on the choice, the chain will connect different sizes of gears, giving the rider many options for power and efficiency. It allows the rider to conquer a steep hill or move at a fast speed when going downhill—all with the same bike. Using the gears well allows riders to adjust their bicycle to the conditions that they are riding in.

MATERIALS

- At least two round plastic or cardboard lids of different sizes. Lids with diameters of about 2 inches (5 cm) and 5 inches (12 cm) work well.
- Scissors or utility knife
- At least 15 individual candies all of the same type, such as spice drops, candy corn, or gumdrops
- Large piece of scrap paper
- Glue (a hot glue gun works well)
- At least two round brads (those things with two bendy prongs that are used to attach paper together)
- Piece of cardboard, at least 8-by-12 inches (20 by 30 cm)
- Permanent marker
- Toothpicks
- Paper
- Adult helper
- A lid with a diameter of about 7 inches (18 cm—optional)
- Additional brads (optional)

PREPARATION

- Start with the larger of your first two container lids to make the disk of your first gear.
- Locate the center of the lid. (Take your time locating the center as this is important to making the gears turn smoothly.)
- Ask an adult to carefully make a small hole in the center of the lid with the scissors or utility knife. Put a brad in the hole, and test whether or not the disk turns freely around the brad. If not, make the hole a little larger and test again.
- Arrange an even number of candies around the rim of the lid, with the base of each candy touching the disk. The candies should be very close together and have no more than a few millimeters of space between them.
- Remove every other candy. This will leave space for the candies (the teeth of the gear) to mesh with candies on another gear.
- Mark the rim of the lid with a dot for each candy so you can remember where to glue them on.
- Lay your lid flat side-down on a piece of scrap paper. Glue the candies to the lid so their sides touch the paper (have an adult help if using a hot glue gun). This ensures the candies, when glued on, form a flat plane.
- Let the glue dry while you repeat this process with the smaller of the first two lids. Prepare at least two lids of different sizes before starting the activity. You can make more later.
- Ensure that the glue is dry and the candies are stable before you start the next steps.

PROCEDURE

- Have an adult help in making a small hole near the middle of your cardboard. You will use this hole to attach the largest of the two gears you prepared to the cardboard.
- Thread a brad through the hole in the larger gear and then through the hole in the cardboard. Bend its arms so the disk is fixed to the board. Test if the disk turns freely around the brad, and make adjustments where needed.
- Place the smaller gear to the left of the larger one so one tooth is interlocked between two teeth of the larger gear. Let the tooth of one gear reach close to the rim of the other gear but not quite touching.
- Mark that location on the cardboard, and have an adult help make a hole there.
- Attach the smaller gear to the cardboard with a brad.
- *What do you think will happen when you turn one of these gears?*
- Try it out! *What happens when you turn one disk? What about turning the other disk?*
- Now try turning the other disk. *Was your prediction correct? Can you tell which disk turned the fastest?*
- To make it easier for you to see how fast the disks turn, use the marker to draw a line connecting the center of these two gears.
- Turn the smaller gear until it completes one full rotation. *How far did the larger gear move? Did it make more than, less than, or exactly one complete turn? Can you tell now which disk turned faster? Why would that happen?*
- *Did you notice in which direction the gears turn? Do both turn in the same direction or in opposite directions? Why would that happen?*

SCIENCE FAIR IDEA

Use a container lid with a bigger diameter than the two you used so far to make an even larger gear. Attach it to the right of the set of gears you have so the teeth mesh. *What do you think will happen if you turn one gear of this set? Can you tell which gear will turn the fastest and which will turn the slowest? Can you predict the direction in which the other two gears will move when you make one turn?*

SCIENCE FAIR IDEA

Make more gears of different and equal sizes and try different combinations.

SCIENCE FAIR IDEA

Count the number of teeth on a set of interlocking gears, and use these numbers to find out how much faster a larger gear rotates when it meshes with a smaller one.

SCIENCE FAIR IDEA

The gears in this activity were all attached to a flat piece of cardboard. *Can you make a configuration where one gear is at a right angle with a second gear?*

SCIENCE FAIR IDEA

The axle is the rod that goes through the middle of a gear. The gears you made in this activity rotate around their axles. Sometimes the gears are fixed to their axle, and the axle turns. *Can you make a system where at least one gear is fixed to an axle? What happens if you glue gears of different sizes to the same axle? When could a configuration like that be helpful?*

SCIENCE FAIR IDEA

Find tools and machines around your home and neighborhood that have gears. *Can you find out why gears are used in these tools?*

OBSERVATIONS AND RESULTS

You probably noticed that the smaller a gear is, the faster it rotates. This happens because smaller gears have fewer teeth. Did you also notice that the direction of rotation is the reverse of the other gear when the gears mesh?

Smaller gears have fewer teeth and thus, compared with larger gears, they rotate through fewer teeth before finishing a full rotation. This allows them to turn faster. Take the example of a gear with 12 teeth connected to a gear with 6 teeth. The gear with 12 teeth turns half as fast because it has twice the number of teeth. The interlocking mechanism guarantees that the same number of teeth pass the point where they mesh. When one gear turns over 6 teeth, the other will turn over 6 teeth as well. When the gear with 6 teeth makes a full turn, the second gear only shifts over 6 of its 12 teeth. It only makes half a turn, so it rotates half as fast.

CLEANUP

You can recycle any cardboard that doesn't have glue on it. Any used materials should go in the trash. You can eat any candy you didn't use!

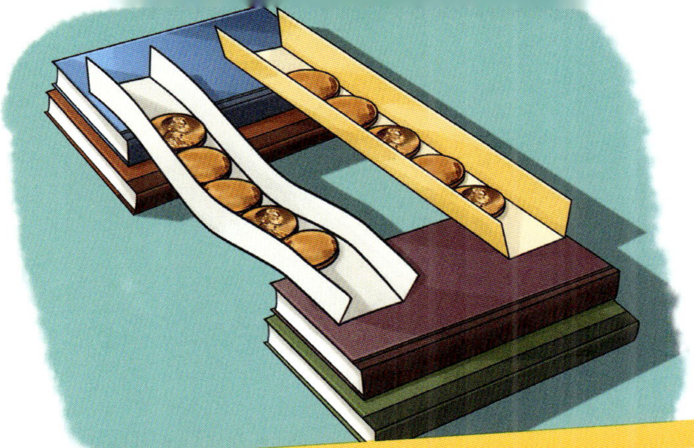

What Material Makes the Strongest Bridge?

BEND OR BREAK? LEARN WHICH MATERIAL MAKES THE BEST BRIDGE—AND A LITTLE BIT ABOUT PHYSICS AND ENGINEERING ALONG THE WAY.

If you've looked at bridges, you've probably noticed that they can be made of different materials. Some are wood, some are steel, some are concrete, and some are even made from stone. If you want to build a simple, sturdy miniature bridge using something you have lying around the house, what's the best material to use? Try this activity to find out!

PROJECT TIME

60 to 90 minutes

KEY CONCEPTS

Physics
Engineering
Materials
Force
Strength

BACKGROUND

What materials should engineers use to build a bridge? The decision depends on many factors. Where is the bridge located? How long will it be? What will go across the bridge (people, cars, or trains) and how heavy will the total load be?

You probably know that different materials have different properties. You might think about the properties of various materials using your senses—for example, how something looks or feels: Is it light or dark, smooth or rough? There are also properties that describe how strong a material is. These are called mechanical properties. For example, how hard is a material to stretch, squish, or bend? When you bend the material and then let go, does it stay bent or go back to its original shape? If you bend the material so far that it breaks, does it happen very slowly or snap suddenly and unexpectedly?

You might have experienced these different properties in everyday life without realizing it. When you bend a paper clip, it stays bent; it's also hard to make the paper clip snap suddenly. Compare that with a wooden ruler. If you were to flex the ruler a little bit, it would bounce back to its original shape; but if you were to bend it too far, it would snap. Some materials, such as rubber, are easy to stretch or squish. Other materials, such as rocks, are much stiffer. You can probably imagine what properties would be important for a bridge. If a heavy truck drives over a bridge, do you want the bridge to sag a lot? Do you want the bridge to return to its original shape after the truck leaves? In this activity, you'll explore these properties with various household materials and decide which one would make the best bridge.

MATERIALS

- Two thick books or small boxes
- Paper
- Wax paper
- Aluminum foil
- Scissors
- Tape
- At least 25 pennies. (If you don't have enough pennies, you can use fewer heavier coins, such as quarters, or other small objects to use as weights, such as small rocks, bolts, and so forth.)
- Ruler or measuring tape (optional)

PREPARATION

- Cut your wax paper and aluminum foil into sheets the same size as the piece of paper.
- Space your books roughly 10 inches (25 cm) apart.
- Fold each of your three sheets of material into a bridge shape. First, fold them in half lengthwise at least twice. Then, fold up the edges to make walls. Tape the edges to prevent the bridges from unfolding. Make sure your bridge is wide enough to hold pennies sitting flat. *Which material do you think will make the sturdiest bridge?*

PROCEDURE

- Rest one of your bridges across the gap between the books.
- Place a penny in the middle of the bridge.
- Keep adding more pennies to the bridge one at a time. Space the pennies evenly along the length of the bridge. This simulates how real people or cars travel across a bridge; they aren't all piled on top of one another.
- Watch the bridge carefully as you keep adding pennies. *Does the bridge hold its shape or start to sag?*
- If you fill the entire surface of the bridge with pennies, start a second layer. Keep adding pennies until the bridge collapses. *How many pennies did it take to make the bridge collapse?*
- Repeat the procedure for each of your other bridge materials. *Which bridge held the most pennies? Did the bridges all collapse in the same way, or did some collapse suddenly while others collapsed gradually?*

SCIENCE FAIR IDEA

Build a fresh bridge from each type of material. Add some pennies to each bridge—but not enough to make it collapse—and then remove the pennies. *Does the bridge completely return to its original shape, or is it permanently deformed?*

SCIENCE FAIR IDEA

The shape of an object also affects its strength. Try changing the geometry of your bridges, adjusting, for example, the width of the bottom or the height of the walls or the number of times you fold each sheet in half. *How does changing the shape affect how many pennies the bridge can hold?*

OBSERVATIONS AND RESULTS

You probably found that paper made the strongest bridge. You might have been surprised to find out that the aluminum foil bridge wasn't the strongest. After all, isn't metal stronger than paper? An object's strength depends not just on its material but also on its dimensions. A thick piece of paper can be harder to bend than a thin piece of metal—and aluminum foil is very thin.

If you watched closely, you also might have noticed that the bridges did not all collapse in the same way. The paper bridge might have started to sag gradually, eventually falling and dropping the coins. The aluminum foil and wax paper bridges might have failed much more suddenly—mostly holding their original shapes and then rapidly collapsing. How would you take this information into account when building a bridge of your own?

CLEANUP

Put away any items you want to use again. Throw out or recycle the rest.

Design a Cell Phone Stand

DREAM IT, DESIGN IT, BUILD IT! USE PHYSICS, ENGINEERING, AND SOME CREATIVITY TO CREATE A HANDY STAND FOR A CELL PHONE.

You've probably seen plenty of smartphone holders or stands. You might use one to prop up a tablet to watch a movie, and maybe your parents have mounted one on the dashboard of their car to hold a phone being used for GPS navigation. But why buy one if you could build it yourself? In this project, you'll use the engineering design process to design, test, and build your own smartphone stand.

PROJECT TIME

90 to 120 minutes

KEY CONCEPTS

Physics
Engineering
Weight
Stiffness
Center of mass

BACKGROUND

Look around you. You're probably surrounded by tons of everyday objects that don't seem very "scientific." Desks, chairs, lamps, doors, pencil holders, et cetera. Many of these objects, however, were probably designed by engineers who had to figure out solutions, such as finding the best building materials; determining the weights the objects need to support; and devising efficient ways to manufacture them. If the engineers do their jobs well, you might never notice—but you certainly would if the chair you were sitting on fell apart or the lamp didn't work!

Engineers design things using the engineering design process, which is different from the scientific method. The exact steps of this process may vary a bit depending on whom you ask, but they generally go something like this:

- Define the problem
- Do background research
- Specify requirements
- Brainstorm solutions
- Build a prototype
- Test the prototype
- Iterate

What does "iterate" mean? It means you might do some of the steps more than once! Things rarely work perfectly on the first try. You might think you have the perfect design for something, then test it and find out it doesn't work at all—so it's back to the drawing board! In this project you will get to try out the engineering design process and design your own cell phone stand.

MATERIALS

- Smartphone or a substitute phone made from cardboard, coins and tape (see "Preparation")
- Assorted office supplies and craft materials, such as cardboard, tape, rubber bands, paper clips, glue, et cetera. (Because this is an engineering design project, there is no specific list of materials required for the activity. You can decide what materials you want to use.)
- Pencil and paper for sketching designs

PREPARATION

- If you don't have a phone available, you can make a substitute phone and design a holder for it. First, cut out a rectangular piece of corrugated cardboard about the same size as a smartphone. To make it heavier, tape a rectangular grid of coins to one side of the cardboard. It should now be about the same size and weight as a phone.

PROCEDURE

- Before you can start designing something, you have to define exactly what problem you're trying to solve. A problem might be, for example, "I need to be able to see a phone's screen to use GPS while I'm driving," or, "I want to be able to prop up a tablet to watch a movie without having to hold it." The best solutions to these different problems probably won't be the same. Figure out exactly what problem you're trying to solve before you continue. In other words, why do you need a phone stand? How will you use it?

- Do some background research. If you have internet access, look around online at designs for different types of cell phone stands. Are there different kinds? How are they different? Do they all serve the same purpose?

- Specify the requirements for your phone stand. These will depend on how you plan to use the stand. For example, do you need it to work for phones of different sizes or just one phone? Do you want the angle of the phone to be adjustable? Do you need to make sure certain buttons or ports on the phone remain accessible? Do you need to be able to type or push buttons on the screen without knocking it over?

- Brainstorm some designs for your phone stand. Make sketches of them on paper and write down the materials you would need to build them. Try to come up with at least three different designs, and then think about how they would meet your requirements. Which one do you think will best meet the requirements?
- Build a prototype of your best design. You might need to start iterating at this point! For example, maybe the parts don't all fit together like you thought they would. If you run into problems when building your prototype, it's okay to modify the design or even switch to a completely different design if you realize it won't work as intended.
- Test your prototype! Try using it yourself or giving it to someone else to try out, and go through various real-world usage scenarios. For example, can you plug in the phone's charging cable? If you push on the phone's screen, does it fall over? You could even try dropping it to see if it breaks. Does your prototype meet all of your requirements?
- If not, then it's back to the drawing board—time to iterate and make changes to your design. Keep iterating until your phone stand meets all your requirements.

SCIENCE FAIR IDEA

Even if your stand meets all your initial requirements, you can still try to improve it. For example, can you make a stand with equivalent performance using fewer materials? In the real world, this would save on manufacturing costs.

OBSERVATIONS AND RESULTS

Did your phone stand work perfectly on the first try? You might have thought you had a perfect design on paper and then been surprised to find out it didn't work as intended. Maybe there wasn't enough friction between your stand and the table, so it slid around too easily. Maybe it was too narrow and fell over when you put the phone in, or maybe the materials you used weren't stiff enough and sagged under the phone's weight. There are plenty of things that could have gone wrong—but that's why you built a prototype and tested it first! That gave you a chance to make changes to your design to make sure it met all your requirements.

Engineers do the same thing—you wouldn't want to design a product, start selling it, and then find out it doesn't work properly. Engineers almost always build and test prototypes before launching a final product. Now that you're familiar with the engineering design process, what will you design next?

CLEANUP

Put the materials you used back where you found them.

Robot, Make Me a Sandwich!

LEARN SOME BREAD-AND-(PEANUT)-BUTTER PROGRAMMING—WITH THIS LOW-TECH LUNCHTIME ACTIVITY.

Have you ever wanted a robot assistant that could do all your household chores? Science fiction has been showing us such robots for decades, but they're still not available! What's taking so long? In this project, you will investigate some of the challenges in programming a "robot" to do a simple household task, such as making a sandwich.

PROJECT TIME

30 to 40 minutes

KEY CONCEPTS

Technology
Logic
Computer programming
Debugging

BACKGROUND

Movies and TV are full of robots that can look, feel, and act like humans. They can fly, talk, run, jump and do many other things. In the real world, however, robots are much more limited. Humans have gotten very good at building machines or making computer programs that can do one specific thing much better or faster than a human can. For example, we have computer programs that can beat humans at games such as chess or TV game shows, including *Jeopardy*. There are robotic arms that can rapidly assemble cars in a factory, much faster and more accurately than people can. You can even buy a robot vacuum cleaner that will automatically clean your floors!

Imagine, however, taking any of those robots and asking it to do a simple household task, such as folding your laundry or cooking dinner. They couldn't do it! They would need to be specifically built and programmed to perform those tasks. In this project you will focus on the programming side of this problem. A computer program is a set of instructions for a computer or robot to follow. Computers are very literal and will follow the instructions exactly, even if you make a mistake when writing the instructions. Things that might seem simple or obvious to a human, such as making a sandwich, will not be obvious at all to a robot. The robot has to be told exactly what to do. In this project, you will write a "program" for a person to make a peanut butter and jelly sandwich. You'll ask the person to think like a robot and take your instructions very literally. Making a sandwich is so simple—this should be easy, right? You might be surprised!

Note: building a robot that can do all the things a human hand can do—such as picking up objects with wildly different shapes without breaking them—is another entire problem on its own. In this project you will ask a volunteer to act like a robot, so you don't have to worry about building one.

MATERIALS

- Bread
- Peanut butter
- Jelly
- Knife
- Plate
- Paper towels
- Volunteer
- Pencil and paper
- Surface that can tolerate a little bit of mess

PREPARATION

- Think about the procedure you follow to make a peanut butter and jelly sandwich. Break it down into a series of steps, one at a time.
- Write this procedure down as a numbered list (step 1, step 2, etc.). Make sure you include *all* the steps, even ones you think are obvious.

PROCEDURE

- Give your written procedure and other materials to your volunteer. Your volunteer probably already knows how to make a peanut butter and jelly sandwich. Explain that you need them to pretend they have never made a sandwich before. You want them to do it by following your written directions exactly. They need to act like a robot and do whatever the instructions tell them to do—even if that results in making a mistake. They also shouldn't assume any steps that are missing.
- Watch carefully as your volunteer follows the procedure. *Do they make any mistakes? If so, at what step(s) of your program?* Write down the step(s) and what problem(s) occurred.
- Now you need to "debug" your program by fixing the bugs, or errors, in the code. Based on your notes on any mistakes you observed, write a new version of your program and ask your volunteer to try again. *Do they make the same mistakes as last time? Are there any new mistakes?*
- Repeat the debugging process until your volunteer successfully makes a normal peanut butter and jelly sandwich. *How many attempts did it take?*

SCIENCE FAIR IDEA

You could also try doing this project with verbal commands instead of written instructions.

SCIENCE FAIR IDEA

Try this project with other household tasks, such as washing dishes, folding laundry, or cleaning your room.

OBSERVATIONS AND RESULTS

You might have been very surprised to find out that at first, your volunteer failed to follow what you thought were a very simple set of instructions. There are a lot of tiny steps you take when making a sandwich that you might do automatically, without giving them much thought, and you could have forgotten to include these in your program. For example, what if your program just said "Spread the peanut butter on the bread"? That seems obvious enough to you. However, your volunteer might have done something silly, like used their fingers to spread peanut butter on the bread bag! But remember, your volunteer is a robot that needs very specific instructions. You didn't specify that they should use a knife to spread the peanut butter, or that they needed to take a piece of bread out of the bag first!

There are a lot of other simple mistakes that can happen during this project—such as using the wrong end of the knife, not taking the lid off a jar first, putting the wrong sides of the pieces of bread against each other, etc. Each time you catch a mistake, you will have to change your program to correct it and try again. It might take several attempts before you can fully debug your program!

CLEANUP

This project might have gotten a little messy if there were a lot of "bugs" in your code! Use damp paper towels to clean up any spilled peanut butter and jelly.

Build an Irrigation System

GO WITH THE FLOW AND LET GRAVITY DO THE WORK AS YOU BUILD AND TEST A SIMPLE IRRIGATION MODEL. HOW FAR CAN YOU GET THE WATER TO GO?

Irrigation, the artificial application of water to crops, has been used by humans for thousands of years. Ancient civilizations built complex irrigation systems without the aid of modern technology or construction equipment. Can you design a model irrigation system using simple household materials? Try this project to find out!

PROJECT TIME

20 to 35 minutes

KEY CONCEPTS

Physics
Engineering
Civil engineering
Water

BACKGROUND

Irrigation systems can be vital for growing crops in areas that do not otherwise receive enough rainfall to sustain them. They are even used in areas that are near natural water sources, such as lakes and rivers, to help evenly distribute water among crops. Modern irrigation systems can rely on heavy construction equipment to dig miles of trenches and pumps that can suck water up from deep underground. Electrical power allows us to distribute water through miles of piping across farm fields.

How did ancient civilizations manage to build irrigation systems thousands of years ago? They took many different approaches. For example, they could divert the natural flow of a river toward their crops, use lakes as reservoirs to store extra water for dry seasons, or rely on gravity-powered systems to channel rainwater coming down a mountainside. In this project, you will build a simple model irrigation system using plastic cups and straws powered by nothing but gravity. Can you design a system that evenly distributes water among different cups, simulating how a real irrigation system would send equal amounts of water to different fields?

MATERIALS

- Paper or plastic cups (at least four; they can be different sizes)
- Drinking straws
- Modeling clay
- Scissors
- Utility or craft knife
- Tap water
- An adult helper
- Work area where it's OK to spill water, such as a sink, bathtub, large plastic tub, or an outdoor area
- Towels if working indoors to clean up any spilled water
- Coins to help weigh the cups down (optional)

PREPARATION

- Have your adult helper use the knife to make two small X-shaped slits about one-third of the way down from the top of a cup, on opposite sides of the cup.
- Get two more cups and make one X-shaped slit in each cup, about one-third of the way up from the bottom, but slightly lower than the slits in the first cup (the slits in the first cup should be higher than the slits in the second two cups). *Why do you think it is important to have the holes at different heights?*

PROCEDURE

- Poke one drinking straw through each slit in the first cup. Then poke the other ends of the straws through the slits in the other cups.
- Use small pieces of modeling clay to form a seal around the straws inside each cup to prevent water from leaking out around it.
- If you have trouble getting the cups to sit flat, put a few coins in the bottom of each one to help weigh them down.
- *Slowly pour water into the central cup. What do you think will happen?* You can pretend this central cup represents a natural water source, such as a river or lake, or an area that receives rainfall. Pretend that the other cups represent locations without water. *What happens when the water reaches the straws? Why?*

SCIENCE FAIR IDEA

There are also some scientific tests you can do based on this project. *What happens if you change the angles of the straws, making them steeper or shallower? Does this change how much water each cup receives? What if you change how fast you pour the water (e.g. pour the water so fast that the first cup fills up before it has time to drain through the straws, vs. pouring the water slowly so it drains through the straws right away)?*

SCIENCE FAIR IDEA

Make this project an engineering design challenge. The instructions only tell you how to build a very simple model irrigation system, but this should be enough to get you started. Here are some additional challenges you can try. Feel free to try using other materials that are not listed in the materials section on page 38.

- *Can you design a bigger irrigation system with more cups that all receive water from the central cup? Can you make sure that they all receive the same amount of water when you pour water into the central cup?*
- *Can you design a "chained" irrigation system, where water passes from one cup to the next? Is it possible to get the same amount of water in each cup? What challenges do you encounter in designing and building this system?*
- *Can you transport water over a longer distance? Can you figure out how to space the cups farther apart than one straw length?*

OBSERVATIONS AND RESULTS

When you pour water into the central cup, it should start flowing into the other cups once it reaches the straws. This occurs because gravity pulls the water through the straws, which are angled downward—because you made the holes in the first cup higher than the holes in the other cups. To get equal amounts of water in each cup, it is important to have the straws in the central cup all at the same height. If one straw is higher than another, the cup it leads to will not receive as much water (or any water at all, depending on how slowly you pour the water—if you pour slowly enough, all of the water might go through the lower straw).

You might experience some leaks through the modeling clay seals, which is why it's a good idea to do this project where it's OK to spill some water!

CLEANUP

Use the towels to soak up any water that spilled on the floor so people don't slip.

Build a Bristlebot That Moves Without Electricity

GO, ROBOT, GO! HOW CAN YOU RACE ROBOTS WITHOUT ANY ELECTRICITY? WITH THE POWER OF VIBRATION. TRY THIS ACTIVITY WITH A FRIEND AND SEE WHO CAN BUILD THE SPEEDIEST VIBROBOT!

Bristlebots are a fun and popular type of robot made from the head of a toothbrush, a small watch battery, and a tiny vibrating motor like the kind found in electric toothbrushes. Although these electronic parts can be hard to find around the house, you can still build bristlebots if you make a simple vibrating table instead. This project will show you how to do it—no electronic parts required!

PROJECT TIME

60 to 90 minutes

KEY CONCEPTS

Engineering
Robotics
Vibration
Design

BACKGROUND

Bristlebots are an easy-to-build version of a type of robot that is more generally called "vibrobots," meaning they are powered by vibrating motion. Have you ever noticed how a cell phone in vibrate mode will move slightly if it rings while sitting on a tabletop, or how you can feel a video game controller rumble in your hands? That happens because these electronic devices have tiny motors inside them with spinning weights. When these weights spin very rapidly, that causes the whole device to vibrate. You can put one of these motors, along with a small battery, on a toothbrush to make a miniature robot.

Unlike larger robots that usually have some level of "intelligence" and steering, the motion of a bristlebot is random as it bounces around. However, you can still exert some control over the motion of a bristlebot by adjusting how exactly you build it. In this project, you will test how using straight or slanted toothbrush bristles can affect the motion of a bristlebot and try to come up with a design that can move faster as well as go straight.

MATERIALS

- Two toothbrushes with straight bristles
- Two toothbrushes with slanted bristles
- Scissors
- Ruler
- Glue or double-sided foam tape
- Medium-size cardboard box, like a cereal box or shoebox
- Three wooden pencils
- Other assorted craft materials: pipe cleaners, toothpicks, Styrofoam, et cetera (optional)

PREPARATION

- Carefully cut off one of the large sides of your cardboard box.
- Cut two smaller squares from another side of the box, about 1.5 inches (4 cm) on each side.

- Have an adult help you cut the heads off all four toothbrushes.
- Make your first bristlebot by gluing or taping the two straight toothbrush heads to one of the cardboard squares. Attach the back side of the toothbrush heads to the cardboard so the bristles touch the ground like little legs for your robot. The brush heads should be parallel to each other.
- Make a second bristlebot the same way, using the slanted toothbrush heads.
- Lay two of your pencils out parallel to each other on a table and place the large piece of cardboard on top of them.
- Place both of your bristlebots on one end of the piece of cardboard.

PROCEDURE

- Now you are ready to make your bristlebots move! Use the eraser end of the third pencil like a drumstick to rapidly but gently tap the large piece of cardboard to make it vibrate.
- *How do your bristlebots move? In which direction do they go? Does one of them move faster or go straight better than the other?*
- Keep tapping the piece of cardboard. *Can you get one bristlebot to make it all the way to the other end? Does their motion change if you adjust how hard or how rapidly you tap the cardboard?*

SCIENCE FAIR IDEA

Decorate your bristlebots! Use colored construction paper and add pipe cleaners or googly eyes—but be careful not to add too much weight or it might slow your robots down!

SCIENCE FAIR IDEA

Think about how you could modify your bristlebot designs. We gave you two very basic designs to get you started, but you do not have to use those. You can build a bristlebot out of any craft or household materials you have available. For example, you don't even have to use toothbrushes. *What happens if you use toothpicks as legs instead? Can you design and build a bristlebot that goes faster and straighter?*

SCIENCE FAIR IDEA

Cut three more long strips of cardboard and use them to make walls for two parallel racetracks on your large piece of cardboard. This will make it easier to race two different designs together at a time because the walls will help force the bristlebots to go straight. Ask some friends to build their own bristlebots and race them against one another!

OBSERVATIONS AND RESULTS

You probably found that your bristlebot with slanted bristles moved faster and went straighter than the one with straight bristles. This is because the bristles are all pointed back in one direction, so when the table vibrates, they push the robot forward. One analogy for how this works is ski poles. If you push down on ski poles that are pointing straight up and down, you will not move. If you push down on ski poles that are angled backward, however, you will move forward.

Because this is an engineering design project, there is no single "right" answer or way to build the "best" bristlebot. You may be able to come up with your own design that works better than the ones described here. Also, you might have some trouble getting your bristlebots to work at first and will need to make some adjustments. (For example, they might not work very well if the toothbrushes are not parallel.) Do not get discouraged if everything does not work great on the first try, and do not be afraid to try your own new ideas!

CLEANUP

Put away any unused materials. You can either throw away your bristlebot or keep it for another race!

Build a Catapult

READY, AIM, FIRE! LEARN ABOUT PHYSICS AS YOU BUILD AND MODIFY YOUR OWN CATAPULT—AND LAUNCH COTTON BALLS THROUGH THE AIR! HOW FAR CAN YOU MAKE YOUR SOFT MISSILES SOAR?

Catapults were mighty handy for pirates in the golden age of piracy (during the 17th century). Medieval knights also used them centuries earlier for taking down massive castle walls. Even Greeks and Romans used catapults about 2,000 years ago! These simple machines are quite handy as long as you know how to aim them! In this science activity, you will try your hand at catapult technology. Can you predict where your missile will land?

PROJECT TIME

50 to 60 minutes

KEY CONCEPTS

Physics
Engineering
Elastic potential energy
Projectile motion

BACKGROUND

A catapult works because energy can be converted from one type to another and transferred from one object to another.

When you prepare the catapult to launch, you add energy to it. This energy is stored in the launching device as potential, or stored, energy. The catapult you are about to make uses elastic potential energy stored in a wooden stick as you bend it. When you let go, this stored energy is released, converted into energy of motion, and transferred to the missile (the launched object), which then flies through the air.

The position of the launching device when the missile becomes airborne is an important parameter of aiming. Does the amount of energy with which you're loading your device factor in as well? Try this activity to find out!

MATERIALS

- Eight craft sticks (popsicle sticks)
- Four or five sturdy rubber bands
- Glue
- Plastic bottle cap to hold a cotton ball
- Cotton ball. If you do not have any available, you can make a small ball by crumbling some paper.
- Small open area. About 11 square feet (1 sq m) will do. It should be a sturdy, flat surface such as a table or floor.

PREPARATION

- Note: The simple catapult described in this project is safe when used with a cotton ball. Shooting hard objects or using other homemade catapults can be dangerous. Make sure any objects you launch are soft and light so as not to harm anyone or cause any damage to objects around you.

- Take six craft sticks and stack them one on top of the other. Secure these sticks together by wrapping rubber bands around both ends of the stack. You will anchor the launching stick to this stack, as described in the next step.
- To add the launching stick, take one stick and attach it perpendicular to the stack you just made, around the middle, so you get a cross shape. You can do this with one or two rubber bands that are crossed in an X over the sticks. If you cross it this way, the sticks will stay nicely perpendicular.
- Next, add the base by attaching a stick to one end of the launching stick with a rubber band. If it were not for the stack of sticks in between, the launching stick would fall flat on top of the base. Now the launching stick and the base form a V shape lying on its side with the stack of sticks in the middle.
- Put your catapult on its base, locate the end of the launching stick that sticks up, and glue the bottle cap there so it forms a small cup to hold the missile.
- Wait until the glue is dry.

PROCEDURE

- Put your catapult in an open area with a sturdy, flat surface, such as a table or an open space on a hard floor. Clear about 11 square feet (1 sq m) of open space for the launched object (the missile) to fly and land.
- Place a cotton ball in the launching cup, push the cup down just a little bit, and let go.
- What happened to the ball? Did it fly? Did it go high or low? Where did it land?
- What do you expect will happen when you push the cup farther down? Will this make it fly higher, farther, both higher and farther, or take the same path but maybe faster?

- Perform a test: Put your cotton ball in the cup, push the cup down farther, release, and observe. You might need to repeat the test a few times to make your observations. It all happens fast! Does your ball fly higher or lower? Does it land farther or nearer when you push down a lot compared with when you push down a little?
- Did you notice in which case you needed to do the most work? Is it when you pushed down a little or when you pushed down farther?
- Try more launches. Do you get similar results each time? Is what you observe what you expected? Can you explain why?

SCIENCE FAIR IDEA

Test what happens if you move the stack of six sticks closer to the launching cup or in the other direction. This will change the position of the launching stick when the missile becomes airborne. *How do you think your change will affect the ball's flight path?*

SCIENCE FAIR IDEA

Build several catapults and play a game with your friends. Use a leftover bottle cap as a target. Place the catapults in a circle about 24 inches (60 cm) away from the cup and see who can score the most goals. Make the circle bigger and see who can adjust their launching technique to best fit the new conditions.

OBSERVATIONS AND RESULTS

Did you see your cotton ball fly higher and farther when you pushed your launching stick farther down?

When you bend your stick, you load your launching stick up with energy. When you let go, this energy is released and converted to energy of motion. Most of this energy transfers to the missile, which shoots through the air.

Pushing the stick down farther takes more effort from you. Maybe you felt you needed to exert more force or work harder to bend the stick farther. Bending farther means more elastic potential energy gets stored in the stick, and when you let go, all this potential energy is converted into energy of motion, so the missile flies through the air at a higher speed. In the case of your catapult, the missile probably flew higher and farther.

CLEANUP

Put away any unused materials. You can keep your catapult for future experiments!

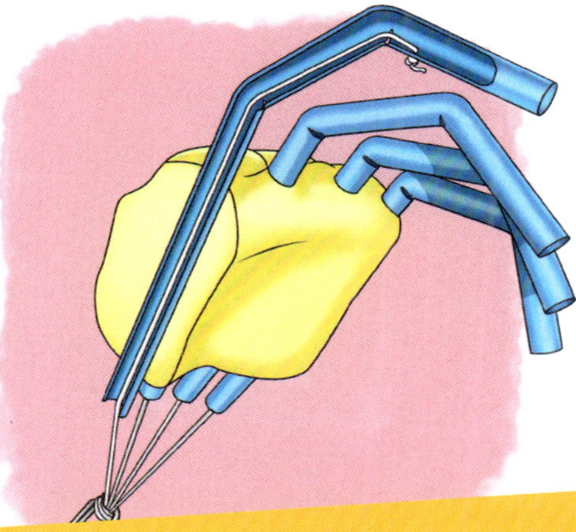

Build an Artificial Hand

BUILD A WORKING HAND THAT YOU CAN CONTROL! WHAT WILL YOU BE ABLE TO PICK UP? FIND OUT—AND LEARN ABOUT ENGINEERING AND ANATOMY—WITH THIS GRIPPING ACTIVITY!

The human hand is pretty amazing. You can do things such as pick up a pencil, use a video game controller, or climb a jungle gym without giving it much thought. Building an artificial hand that can do all those things is quite a challenge! In this project, you will try to build a simple artificial gripper that can pick up small objects.

PROJECT TIME

120 to 150 minutes

KEY CONCEPTS

Engineering
Robotics
Anatomy
Gripping

BACKGROUND

The human hand has five fingers, each with multiple joints. These joints are controlled by muscles and tendons—the muscles pull on the tendons, which pull on the joints and make them bend. The human hand has so many different joints, which makes it very flexible and versatile and easily adaptable to a wide variety of different tasks. You learn to use your hands as a small child, and by the time you grow up, you barely have to think about it at all!

Engineers have been trying to build robotic hands for years, but it turns out that this is very difficult. We have gotten pretty good at building robotic hands that are good at one specific thing. For example, a robotic gripper in a factory might be designed to pick up a certain part and bolt it onto a car. If you try to get that gripper to pick up a tennis ball or a glass of water, however, it will not work at all! Building a mechanical hand that is as versatile as the human hand remains a huge challenge.

In this project, you will build a simple artificial gripper using drinking straws and string. You will cut notches in the straws that will act as the "joints" and thread strings through the straws to act as the "tendons." Pulling on the strings will cause the joints to bend. You can experiment with building different types of grippers, such as a simple clawlike gripper that just has two fingers with one joint each or a full humanlike hand with individual control of multiple joints.

MATERIALS

- Plastic drinking straws
- Needle (Use caution and adult help when handling sharp objects.)
- String
- Paper clips
- Modeling clay
- Assorted small objects to pick up
- Scissors
- Tweezers (optional)
- Small rubber bands (optional)
- Paper towel tube (optional)

PREPARATION

- Assemble all your materials on a flat working space that has enough area to make and test your creation.

PROCEDURE

- First you will practice making a single "finger." Use scissors (and adult assistance if necessary) to carefully cut a small triangular notch in the middle of a drinking straw. Make sure you do not cut the whole way through the straw. This should allow you to kink the straw at that point, but after you let go, the straw should snap back to its original shape. This notch is the "joint" in your finger.

- Tie one end of the string through the eye of the needle.

- Carefully puncture the straw with the needle, just above the notch you cut out. Make sure you puncture the straw on the same side that you cut out the notch, not on the "back" side.

- Push the needle all the way into the straw past the notch you cut out and thread it out the bottom of the straw. It might help to use a pair of tweezers to reach into the straw (either through the notch, or from the bottom) to grab the needle and pull it through. You can also hold the straw vertically and shake it to let the needle fall down.

- Keep pulling the needle through until about 4 inches (10 cm) of string comes out the bottom of the straw. This string will act like a "tendon" that helps the finger bend.

- Cut the other end of the string, leaving enough extra that you can tie off a knot. Make sure the knot is large enough that it cannot be pulled through the hole you punctured with the needle.

- Untie or cut off the string from the eye of the needle.

- Tie the bottom end of the string to a paper clip.
- You have just completed your first "finger." Hold the base of the straw with one hand. Pull on the paper clip with your other hand. This should cause the straw to bend at the notch, similar to a finger bending at a joint. *What could you pick up with just this one finger? How would having more fingers help?*
- Now it's time to build more fingers! Repeat the above steps to make at least one more finger. You can also decide whether each finger has multiple joints or just one. If a finger does have multiple joints, you can use a single string to control all of them (by tying it off above the last joint) or individual strings to control each one (by threading multiple strings through the straw above each joint).
- Play around with making different types of fingers and controlling them by pulling on the strings.
- Now it's time to link up some fingers into a gripper! The type of hand you design and build is totally up to you. Keep in mind that you do not have to design a human hand with five fingers. For example, you could make a claw with two pincers (like a crab or lobster), or a claw with three or four symmetric fingers (like the kind in arcade machines that pick up a stuffed animal).
- Try combining multiple fingers. Use modeling clay to form the base or "palm" of your hand by forming it around the base of the straws. Make sure you do not cover the bottom opening of the straws so you can still pull on the string. Adjusting the modeling clay allows you to change the position and orientation of the fingers relative to one another.
- Depending on the type of modeling clay you have, you may want to let it air-dry and harden so your hand will work better. (It might be difficult to work with the hand while the clay is still mushy. Some types of clay might be hard enough to begin with so that they will work right away.)

- Try pulling on the string(s) to control the fingers once they are mounted in the palm of your hand. You might need to make some adjustments to get everything working properly. *What changes do you think you can make to improve the performance of your hand?*
- Now try using your hand to pick up some small objects. Keep in mind that your hand is made of straws; it is not very strong, so you should only use it to pick up lightweight objects (for example, empty plastic bottles, not ones full of liquid).
- *Is your hand better at picking up certain objects than others? Could you design a hand that is specifically designed to snatch certain objects? For example, one type of hand to pick up cylindrical objects like bottles and another type to grab spherical objects like tennis balls? Do you think it would be hard to design something as adaptive as the human hand, which can easily pick up things with very different shapes?*

SCIENCE FAIR IDEA

Mount the palm of your mechanical hand on the end of a cardboard paper towel tube and thread the strings through the tube. Now you have a gripper with an extended reach that you can use to pick things up!

SCIENCE FAIR IDEA

Plastic straws can be somewhat slippery, so try to improve the "grip" of your mechanical hand. For example, wrap small rubber bands around the straws. *Does improving the "grip" of the straws make it easier to pick things up?*

OBSERVATIONS AND RESULTS

You should be able to build an artificial hand that can pick up light objects, such as ping-pong balls, empty plastic bottles, or small stuffed animals. It will be difficult to build a hand out of straws and modeling clay that can grab heavier objects. If you want to build a stronger hand, you might be able to replace the straws and clay with sturdier materials from a hardware store (for example, plastic piping for the fingers, metal cable for the tendons, and a wooden base with holes drilled in it for the palm).

It is much easier to build and control a hand where all the fingers and joints are controlled by a single string (similar to the "arcade machine"-style claw, where all the fingers open and close at once). It is much more difficult to build an articulated hand with multiple joints that are controlled individually—but that should not discourage you from trying! Remember, your own hands are very complicated, and professional engineers are still struggling to this day to build a fully functional robotic hand that is equivalent to a human one.

Because this is an engineering design activity, there is no specific formula to follow in building your hand. Designs can be very different, and there is no "right" or "wrong" way to make it. You might find some designs to be better at performing different functions. If you built different hands with different numbers of fingers, which one did you find to be the most versatile?

CLEANUP

Throw away or recycle any scraps you didn't use.

THE SCIENTIFIC METHOD

The scientific method helps scientists—and students—gather facts to prove whether an idea is true. Using this method, scientists come up with ideas and then test those ideas by observing facts and drawing conclusions. You can use the scientific method to develop and test your own ideas!

Question: What do you want to learn? What problem needs to be solved? Be as specific as possible.

Research: Learn more about your topic and refine your question.

Hypothesis: Form an educated guess about what you think will answer your question. This allows you to make a prediction you can test.

Experiment: Create a test to learn if your hypothesis is correct. Limit the number of variables, or elements of the experiment that could change.

Analysis: Record your observations about the progress and results of your experiment. Then analyze your data to understand what it means.

Conclusion: Review all your data. Did the results of the experiment match the prediction? If so, your hypothesis was correct. If not, your hypothesis may need to be changed.

GLOSSARY

analogy: A comparison of things based on ways they are alike.

anatomy: A science that has to do with the structure of living things.

artificial: Made by humans.

automate: To run or operate something using machines instead of people.

civil engineering: Engineering work that is done for use by everyday citizens, rather than the military.

contaminate: To make unfit for use by adding something harmful or unpleasant.

diameter: A straight line that runs from one side of a figure and passes through the center.

efficient: Able to bring about a desired result with little waste of time or energy.

exert: To make an effort.

friction: Resistance to motion between objects in contact.

processing: Changing by a special treatment.

manually: By hand, without the help of machines.

mesh: To fit or join together.

physics: A science that deals with matter and energy and their interactions.

projectile: Something thrown or shot.

simulate: To give something the appearance or effect of something else.

symmetrical: Arranged in a way that involves regular and balanced proportions.

tendon: A band of tough white fiber connecting a muscle to another body part, especially bone.

versatile: Having many different uses.

ADDITIONAL RESOURCES

Books

Hynson, Colin. *Amazing Engineering Jobs*. London, UK: Wayland, 2019.

Schutte, Sarah L. *10-Minute Engineering Projects*. North Mankato, MN: Capstone Press, 2020.

Thompson, Veronica. *Earth-Friendly Engineering Crafts*. Minneapolis, MN: Lerner Publications, 2019.

Websites

Discovery Education
sciencefaircentral.com

Exploratorium
https://www.exploratorium.edu/search/science%20fair%20projects

Science Buddies
https://www.sciencebuddies.org/science-fair-projects/project-ideas/list

Science Fun
https://www.sciencefun.org/?s=science+fair

Videos

"3-D Mapping Your World with a Backpack."
https://ny.pbslearningmedia.org/resource/77c0bb79-a2aa-462d-90ae-e32c3e440351/3-d-mapping-your-world-with-a-backpack-engineering-is/. PBS Learning Media, 4:58.

"Career Spotlight: Spatial Interaction Engineer."
https://ny.pbslearningmedia.org/resource/a85be67d-eb84-4d0a-8a70-b89daa9eb61a/career-spotlight-spatial-interaction-engineer/. PBS Learning Media, 2:51.

INDEX